The Phrase by Phrase translation of the Matn of Nawaqid al Islam and Qawaaidul Arbaa

Dr. Muddassir Khan

In the Name of Allaah,
The Most Merciful,
The Bestower of Mercy.

Table of Contents

01: Nullifiers of Faith

نواقض الإسلام

بِسْمِ اللَّهِ الرَّحْمَنِ الرَّحِيمِ

In the Name of Allaah, the Most Merciful, the
Bestower of Mercy.

اعْلَمْ أَنَّ نَوَاقِضِ الإِسْلَامِ عَشَرَةً

Know that the Nullifiers of Islaam are ten:

الأَوَّلُ: الشِّرْكُ فِي عِبَادَةِ اللَّه تَعَالَى؛

The first: Shirk (major shirk: the association of partners) in the worship of Allah, the Most High

وَالدَّلِيلُ قَوْلُهُ تَعَالَى

And the proof is His saying, the Most High:

{إِنَّ اللَّهَ لَا يَغْفِرُ أَن يُشْرَكَ بِهِ وَيَغْفِرُ مَا دُونَ ذَلِكَ لِمَن يَشَاءُ}،

"Verily, Allaah does not forgive that partners be set up with Him (in worship), but He forgives whatever is less than that (anything else) to whom He pleases..."

(Soorah An-Nisa' 4:48)

وَمِنْهُ: الذَّبْحُ لِغَيْرِ اللَّهِ؛ كَمَنْ يَذْبَحُ لِلْجِنِّ، أَوْ لِلْقَبْرِ

From it is slaughtering for other than Allaah; such as the one who slaughters for the jinn or for the one (who is dead) in the grave.

الثَّانِي: مَنْ جَعَلَ بَيْنَهُ وَبَيْنَ اللَّهِ وَسَائِطَ،

The Second: Whoever sets up intermediaries (al-Wasaa'it) between himself and Allah,

يَدْعُوهُمْ، وَيَسْأَلُهُمُ الشَّفَاعَةَ، وَيَتَوَكَّلُ عَلَيْهِمْ؛

supplicating to them (ad-Du'aa), asking them for

intercession (Shafaa'a), and relying upon them (Tawakkul),

كَفَرَ إِجْمَاعاً.

has disbelieved (has already become an Unbeliever) by way of unanimous agreement (*Ijmaa'* – consensus of the people of knowledge).

الثَّالِثُ: مَنْ لَمْ يُكَفِّرِ المُشْرِكِينَ،

The third: He who does not deem the polytheists to be disbelievers,

أَوْ شَكَّ فِي كُفْرِهِمْ،

or doubts their disbelief,

أَوْ صَحَّحَ مَذْهَبَهُمْ؛

or deems their path (*madh-hab* - way of life/religion) to be correct

كَفَرَ إِجْمَاعاً.

has disbelieved according to *Ijmaa* (consensus).

الرَّابِعُ: مَنِ اعْتَقَدَ أَنَّ غَيْرَ هَدْيِ النَّبِيِّصَلَّى اللهُ عَلَيْهِ وَسَلَّمَ أَكْمَلُ مِنْ هَدْيِهِ،

The Fourth: The one who believes that guidance other than the Prophet's (peace and blessings of Allaah be upon him) is more complete (perfect) than his guidance;

أَوْ أَنَّ حُكْمَ غَيْرِهِ أَحْسَنُ مِنْ حُكْمِهِ –

or that a judgment (Ruling) other than his is superior to (better than) his judgment

كَالَّذِينَ يُفَضِّلُونَ حُكْمَ الطَّوَاغِيتِ عَلَى حُكْمِهِ –

such as he who prefers the judgment of the Tawaagheet (that other than Allaah which is worshipped, followed, or obeyed) over his judgment.

فَهُوَ كَافِرٌ.

then he is a disbeliever.

الخَامِسُ: مَنْ أَبْغَضَ شَيْئاً مِمَّا جَاءَ بِهِ
الرَّسُولُ صَلَّى اللهُ عَلَيْهِ وَسَلَّمَ-

The Fifth: He who hates anything which the Messenger (peace and blessings of Allaah be upon him) came with,

وَلَوْ عَمِلَ بِهِ -؛

even if he acts upon it,

كَفَرَ إِجْمَاعاً؛

has disbelieved by *Ijmaa*.

وَالدَّلِيلُ قَوْلُهُ تَعَالَى:

and the proof of this is the saying of Allaah, the
Most High:

{ذَلِكَ بِأَنَّهُمْ كَرِهُوا مَا أَنزَلَ اللَّهُ فَأَحْبَطَ أَعْمَالَهُمْ}.

That is because they hate that which Allaah has sent
down (this Quraan, Islamic laws, etc.), so He has
made their deeds fruitless.

(Surah Muhammad 47:9)

السَّادِسُ: مَنِ اسْتَهْزَأَ بِشَيْءٍ مِنْ دِينِ اللهِ،

The Sixth: He who mocks anything from the religion of Allaah,

أَوْ ثَوَابِهِ، أَوْ عِقَابِهِ؛

or His reward, or His punishment,

كَفَرَ؛

he has disbelieved.

وَالدَّلِيلُ قَوْلُهُ تَعَالَى:

The proof is the statement of Allaah, the Most-High:

{قُلْ أَبِاللَّهِ وَآيَاتِهِ وَرَسُولِهِ كُنتُمْ تَسْتَهْزِئُونَ * لَا تَعْتَذِرُوا قَدْ كَفَرْتُم بَعْدَ إِيمَانِكُمْ}.

Say: "Was it at Allaah, and His Ayaat (proofs, signs, and revelations) and His Messenger (peace and blessings of Allaah be upon him) that you were mocking? Make no excuse; you have disbelieved after you had believed..."

(At-Tawbah 9:65-66)

السَّابِعُ: السِّحْرُ - وَمِنْهُ: الصَّرْفُ وَالعَطْفُ -

The Seventh: Magic. From it is As-Sarf (causing alienation) and Al-'Atf (causing affection or attachment).

فَمَنْ فَعَلَهُ أَوْ رَضِيَ بِهِ؛ كَفَرَ؛

He who does it or is pleased with it has disbelieved.

وَالدَّلِيلُ قَوْلُهُ تَعَالَى:

The proof is the statement of Allaah, the Most-High:

{وَمَا يُعَلِّمَانِ مِنْ أَحَدٍ حَتَّى يَقُولَا إِنَّمَا نَحْنُ فِتْنَةٌ فَلَا تَكْفُرْ}.

But neither of these two (angels Haaroot and Maaroot) taught anyone (such things) till they had said, "We are only for trial (*fitnah*), so disbelieve not (by learning this magic from us)."

الثَّامِنُ: مُظَاهَرَةُ المُشْرِكِينَ وَمُعَاوَنَتُهُمْ عَلَى المُسْلِمِينَ؛

The Eight: Giving victory to (backing) the polytheists and aiding them against the Muslims.

وَالدَّلِيلُ قَوْلُهُ تَعَالَى:

The proof is the statement of Allaah, the Most-High:

﴿وَمَن يَتَوَلَّهُم مِّنكُمْ فَإِنَّهُ مِنْهُمْ إِنَّ اللَّهَ لَا يَهْدِي الْقَوْمَ الظَّالِمِينَ﴾.

And if any amongst you has allegiance with them (the infidels), then surely he is one of them. Verily, Allaah guides not those people who are wrongdoers.

(Al-Ma'idah 5:51)

التَّاسِعُ: مَنِ اعْتَقَدَ أَنَّ بَعْضَ النَّاسِ يَسَعُهُ الخُرُوجُ عَنْ شَرِيعَتِ مُحَمَّدٍ - صَلَّى اللهُ عَلَيْهِ وَسَلَّمَ-

The Ninth: He who believes that some of the people are allowed to depart from the legislation of Muhammad (peace and blessings of Allaah be upon him)

كَمَا وَسِعَ الخَضِرَ الخُرُوجُ عَنْ شَرِيعَةِ مُوسَى

- عَلَيْهِ السَّلَامُ؛ فَهُوَ كَافِرٌ.

just as Al-Khadir departed from the legislation of Moosaa (peace be upon him) then he is a disbeliever.

العَاشِرُ: الإِعْرَاضُ عَنْ دِينِ اللَّهِ - لَا يَتَعَلَّمُهُ وَلَا يَعْمَلُ بِهِ -؛

The Tenth: Turning away from the religion of Allaah (the Most-High); by neither learning it nor acting upon it.

وَالدَّلِيلُ قَوْلُهُ تَعَالَى:

The proof is the statement of Allaah, the Most High:

{وَمَنْ أَظْلَمُ مِمَّن ذُكِّرَ بِآيَاتِ رَبِّهِ ثُمَّ أَعْرَضَ عَنْهَا إِنَّا مِنَ الْمُجْرِمِينَ مُنتَقِمُونَ}.

And who does more wrong than he who is reminded of the Ayaat (proofs, evidences, verses, signs, revelations, etc.) of his Lord, then he turns away therefrom? Verily, We shall exact retribution from the criminals.

(As-Sajdah 32:22)

Conclusion

وَلَا فَرْقَ فِي جَمِيعِ هَذِهِ النَّوَاقِضِ بَيْنَ الهَازِلِ وَالجَادِّ وَالخَائِفِ،

There is no difference regarding all of these (nullifiers) between the one who is joking (*al-Haazil*), serious (*al-Jaadd*), or scared (al-Khaa'if),

إِلَّا المُكْرَه.

with the exception of the one who is compelled (al-Mukrah).

وَكُلُّهَا مِنْ أَعْظَمِ مَا يَكُونُ خَطَرًا،

All of these (nullifiers) are from the most dangerous (matters),

وَمِنْ أَكْثَرِ مَا يَكُونُ وُقُوعاً،

and the most frequently fallen into.

فَيَنْبَغِي لِلْمُسْلِمِ أَنْ يَحْذَرَهَا وَيَخَافَ مِنْهَا عَلَى نَفْسِهِ.

Therefore, it is befitting for the Muslim to beware (be cautious) of them and to fear them for himself (from falling into them).

نَعُوذُ بِاللَّهِ مِنْ مُوجِبَاتِ غَضَبِهِ، وَأَلِيمِ عِقَابِه.

We seek refuge with Allaah (the Most-High) from
that which brings about His anger and His painful
punishment.

وَصَلَّى اللَّهُ عَلَى نَبِيِّنَا مُحَمَّدٍ، وَعَلَى آلِهِ
وَصَحْبِهِ وَسَلَّمَ.

May the blessings and peace from Allaah be upon
the best of His creation, Muhammad, his family,
and companions.

* * *

02: Al-Qawaaid al-Arbaa

القواعد الأربع

بِسْمِ اللَّهِ الرَّحْمَنِ الرَّحِيمِ

In the Name of Allaah, the Most Merciful, the
Bestower of Mercy.

أَسْأَلُ اللَّهَ الْكَرِيمَ، رَبَّ الْعَرْشِ الْعَظِيمِ:

"I ask Allaah, the Most Generous, Lord of the Great
(Majestic) Throne

أَنْ يَتَوَلَّاكَ فِي الدُّنْيَا وَالْآخِرَةِ،

to befried you (takes charge of your affairs) in this world and the Hereafter,

وَأَنْ يَجْعَلَكَ مُبَارَكاً أَيْنَمَا كُنْتَ.

and to make you blessed whereever you are.

وَأَنْ يَجْعَلَكَ مِمَّن إِذَا أُعْطِيَ شَكَرَ،

And (I ask) that He make you from those who when they are given, (they) are thankful;

وَإِذَا ابْتُلِيَ صَبَرَ،

when they are tested, (they) are patient;

وَإِذَا أَذْنَبَ اسْتَغْفَرَ؛

and when they sin, (they) seek forgiveness (from Allaah, that is they repent).

فَإِنَّ هَؤُلَاءِ الثَّلَاثَ عُنْوَانُ السَّعَادَةِ.

For indeed these three characteristics (signs) are the true signs of happiness (success)."

اعْلَمْ - أَرْشَدَكَ اللهُ لِطَاعَتِهِ -: أَنَّ الحَنِيفِيَّةَ - مِلَّةَ إِبْرَاهِيمَ-:

"Know, may Allaah grant you the ability to obey Him(guide you to His obedience), that the Haneefiyyah (Monotheism), the religion of Ibraaheem

أَنْ تَعْبُدَ اللَّهَ وَحْدَهُ مُخْلِصاً لَهُ الدِّينَ،

is that you worship (only) Allaah alone, making the Religion sincere for only Him (being sincere to Him in the religion),

وَبِذَلِكَ أَمَرَ اللَّهُ جَمِيعَ النَّاسِ، وَخَلَقَهُمْ لَهَا؛

this is what Allaah commands the people with and created them for,

كَمَا قَالَ تَعَالَى:

as Allaah says

{ وَمَا خَلَقْتُ الْجِنَّ وَالْإِنسَ إِلَّا لِيَعْبُدُونِ.}

"And I did not create the Jinn and mankind except to worship Me."

[Suratudh-Dhaariyaat, Verse 56]

فَإِذَا عَرَفْتَ أَنَّ اللَّهَ خَلَقَكَ لِعِبَادَتِهِ:

So, when you come to realize that Allaah created you in order to worship Him (for His Ibaadah),

فَاعْلَمْ أَنَّ الْعِبَادَةَ لَا تُسَمَّى عِبَادَةً إِلَّا مَعَ التَّوْحِيدِ،

then know that worship (ibaadah) is not called worship unless it is accompanied by Tawheed (singling out Allaah alone with worship),

كَمَا أَنَّ الصَّلَاةَ لَا تُسَمَّى صَلَاةً إِلَّا مَعَ الطَّهَارَةِ.

just as prayer (Salah) is not called that unless it is accompanied by (ritual) purity (tahaarah).

فَإِذَا دَخَلَ الشِّرْكُ فِي العِبَادَةِ فَسَدَتْ،

So if Shirk (associating partners with Allaah in His worship) enters into one's worship, it ruins it,

كَالحَدَثِ إِذَا دَخَلَ فِي الطَّهَارَةِ؛

just like impurity (hadath) when it enters into the (ritual) purity.

كَمَا قَالَ تَعَالَى:

As Allaah said:

﴿مَا كَانَ لِلْمُشْرِكِينَ أَن يَعْمُرُوا مَسَاجِدَ اللَّهِ شَاهِدِينَ عَلَى أَنفُسِهِم بِالْكُفْرِ أُوْلَئِكَ حَبِطَتْ أَعْمَالُهُمْ وَفِي النَّارِ هُمْ خَالِدُونَ﴾

It is not for the Mushrikoon (polytheists, idolaters, pagans, disbelievers in the Oneness of Allaah), to maintain the Mosques of Allâh (i.e. to pray and worship Allaah therein, to look after their cleanliness and their building,), while they witness against their ownselves of disbelief. The works of such are in vain and in Fire shall they abide.

فَإِذَا عَرَفْتَ أَنَّ الشِّرْكَ إِذَا خَالَطَ الْعِبَادَةَ أَفْسَدَهَا،

So when you come to realize that Shirk – when mixed into one's worship – spoils (destroys) it,

وَأَحْبَطَ الْعَمَلَ،

invalidates (destroys) one's actions,

وَصَارَ صَاحِبُهُ مِنَ الْخَالِدِينَ فِي النَّارِ:

and makes the person who possesses it into one who will reside eternally (forever) in the Hellfire,

عَرَفْتَ أَنَّ أَهَمَّ مَا عَلَيْكَ مَعْرِفَةُ ذَلِكَ؛

you will know that the most important thing that is

binding upon you is to gain knowledge of that
(shirk),

لَعَلَّ اللَّهَ أَنْ يُخَلِّصَكَ مِنْ هَذِهِ الشَّبَكَةِ،

so that perhaps Allaah may absolve you from this
trap,

وَهِيَ الشِّرْكُ بِاللَّهِ.

which is ascribing partners to Allaah (i.e. Shirk).

وَذَلِكَ بِمَعْرِفَةِ أَرْبَعِ قَوَاعِدَ ذَكَرَهَا اللَّهُ تَعَالَى فِي كِتَابِهِ:

And this can be achieved by knowing four principles that Allaah

mentioned in His book.

القَاعِدَةُ الأُولَى

THE FIRST PRINCIPLE:

أَنْ تَعْلَمَ: أَنَّ الكُفَّارَ الَّذِينَ قَاتَلَهُمْ رَسُولُ الله صَلَّى اللهُ عَلَيْهِ وَسَلَّمَ

That you know that verily the disbelievers that the

مُقِرُّونَ أَنَّ اللَّهَ هُوَ الخَالِقُ الرَّازِقُ، المُحْيِي المُمِيتُ، المُدَبِّرُ لِجَمِيعِ الأُمُورِ،

do affirm that surely Allaah, the exalted is the creator, the provider, the giver of life, the inflicter of death, the manager of all matters (the Administrator),

وَلَمْ يُدْخِلْهُمْ ذَلِكَ فِي الإِسْلَامِ؛

and that this (but their affirmation – this belief) does not enter them into Islaam.

وَالدَّلِيلُ قَوْلُهُ تَعَالَى :

The proof for this is Allaah's saying:

{قُلْ مَن يَرْزُقُكُم مِّنَ السَّمَاءِ وَالْأَرْضِ أَمَّن يَمْلِكُ السَّمْعَ وَالْأَبْصَارَ وَمَن يُخْرِجُ الْحَيَّ مِنَ الْمَيِّتِ وَيُخْرِجُ الْمَيِّتَ مِنَ الْحَيِّ وَمَن يُدَبِّرُ الْأَمْرَ فَسَيَقُولُونَ اللَّهُ فَقُلْ أَفَلَا تَتَّقُونَ}.

Say (O Muhammad ﷺ): "Who provides for you from the sky and from the earth? Or who owns hearing and sight? And who brings out the living from the dead and brings out the dead from the living? And who disposes the affairs?" They will say: "Allaah." Say: "Will you not then be afraid of Allaah's Punishment (for setting up rivals in worship with Allaah)?"

(Surah Yunus 10:31)

القَاعِدَةُ الثَّانِيَةُ

THE SECOND PRINCIPLE:

أَنَّهُمْ يَقُولُونَ: مَا دَعَوْنَاهُمْ وَتوجَّهْنَا إِلَيْهِمْ، إِلَّا لِطَلَبِ القُرْبَةِ وَالشَّفَاعَةِ.

That verily, they (the polytheists) say; we don't invoke them (the false deities) and turn towards them except to seek closeness (to Allaah) and intercession.

فَدَلِيلُ القُرْبَةِ؛ قَوْلُهُ تَعَالى:

The proof for (their claim of seeking) closeness is
the word of Allaah:

{وَالَّذِينَ اتَّخَذُوا مِن دُونِهِ أَوْلِيَاءَ مَا نَعْبُدُهُمْ إِلَّا لِيُقَرِّبُونَا إِلَى اللَّهِ زُلْفَى إِنَّ اللَّهَ يَحْكُمُ بَيْنَهُمْ فِي مَا هُمْ فِيهِ يَخْتَلِفُونَ إِنَّ اللَّهَ لَا يَهْدِي مَنْ هُوَ كَاذِبٌ كَفَّارٌ}.

"And those who take protectors besides Him (say):
'We don't worship them except to bring us closer
to Allaah.' Verily Allaah will judge between them
concerning that which they differ in. Verily, Allaah
does not guide he who is a liar, a disbeliever."

وَدَلِيلُ الشَّفَاعَةِ؛ قَوْلُهُ تَعَالَى:

The proof for their (claim of) seeking intercession is Allaah's saying:

$$\{ \text{وَيَعْبُدُونَ مِن دُونِ اللَّهِ مَا لَا يَضُرُّهُمْ وَلَا يَنفَعُهُمْ وَيَقُولُونَ هَؤُلَاءِ شُفَعَاؤُنَا عِندَ اللَّهِ قُلْ أَتُنَبِّئُونَ اللَّهَ بِمَا لَا يَعْلَمُ فِي السَّمَاوَاتِ وَلَا فِي الْأَرْضِ سُبْحَانَهُ وَتَعَالَى عَمَّا يُشْرِكُونَ} \}$$

And they worship besides Allaah things that harm them not nor benefit them. And they say: 'These are our intercessors besides Allaah.' Say: 'Do you inform Allaah of that which He knows not in the heavens and on the earth?' Glorified and Exalted is He above all that which they associate as partners (with Him)!

وَالشَّفَاعَةُ شَفَاعَتَانِ: شَفَاعَةٌ مَنْفِيَّةٌ، وَشَفَاعَةٌ مُثْبَتَةٌ.

And intercession is of two types: Intercession that is negated and Intercession that is affirmed.

فَالشَّفَاعَةُ المَنْفِيَّةُ: مَا كَانَتْ تُطْلَبُ مِنْ غَيْرِ اللهِ فِيمَا لَا يَقْدِرُ عَلَيْهِ إِلَّا اللهُ؛

As for the negated intercession: it is that which is sought from (someone) other than Allaah in that which no one has power over (it) (ability to carry out) except Allaah.

وَالدَّلِيلُ قَوْلُهُ تَعَالَى:

And the proof is the word of Allaah:

{يَاأَيُّهَا الَّذِينَ آمَنُوا أَنفِقُوا مِمَّا رَزَقْنَاكُم مِّن قَبْلِ أَن يَأْتِيَ يَوْمٌ لَّا بَيْعٌ فِيهِ وَلَا خُلَّةٌ وَلَا شَفَاعَةٌ وَالْكَافِرُونَ هُمُ الظَّالِمُونَ}.

O you who believe! Spend of that with which we have provided for you, before a Day comes when there will be no bargaining, nor friendship, nor intercession. And it is the disbelievers who are the Zalimun (wrong-doers, etc.)." [Soorah al-Baqarah, verse: 254]

وَالشَّفَاعَةُ المُثْبَتَةُ: هِيَ الَّتِي تُطْلَبُ مِنَ اللَّهِ.

And as for the affirmed intercession: it is that which is sought from Allaah.

وَالشَّافِعُ مُكْرَمٌ بِالشَّفَاعَةِ.

And the intercessor (is the one who) is honored with the intercession (the honor of being able to intercede with the permission of Allaah),

وَالمَشْفُوعُ لَهُ: مَنْ رَضِيَ اللَّهُ قَوْلَهُ وَعَمَلَهُ بَعْدَ الإِذْنِ؛

and the one for whom intercession is sought (the one who is interceded) for is the one whom Allaah is pleased with his speech and actions, (and all of these occur) after the permission (from Allaah),

كَمَا قَالَ تَعَالَى:

as Allaah

said:

{مَن ذَا الَّذِي يَشْفَعُ عِندَهُ إِلَّا بِإِذْنِهِ}.

Who is he that can intercede with Him except with
His Permission?

[Soorah al-Baqarah, verse: 255]

القَاعِدَةُ الثَّالِثَةُ

THE THIRD PRINCIPLE:

أَنَّ النَّبِيَّ صَلَّى اللهُ عَلَيْهِ وَسَلَّمَ ظَهَرَ عَلَى أُنَاسٍ مُتَفَرِّقِينَ فِي عِبَادَاتِهِمْ:

That verily the Prophet ﷺ appeared (was sent) amongst (to)

people who are different in their worships (who differed from one another in their worship),

مِنْهُمْ: مَنْ يَعْبُدُ الشَّمْسَ وَالقَمَرَ.

from them is one who worships the sun and moon.

وَمِنْهُمْ: مَنْ يَعْبُدُ المَلَائِكَةَ.

from them is one who worships the angels.

وَمِنْهُمْ: مَنْ يَعْبُدُ الأَنْبِيَاءَ وَالصَّالِحِينَ.

from them is one who worships the prophets and the righteous.

وَمِنْهُمْ: مَنْ يَعْبُدُ الأَشْجَارَ وَالأَحْجَارَ.

from them is one who worships trees and stones.

وَقَاتَلَهُمْ رَسُولُ صَلَّى اللهُ عَلَيْهِ وَسَلَّمَ،

So the Messenger of Allaah ﷺ fought them all

وَلَمْ يُفَرِّقْ بَيْنَهُمْ؛

and he did not make any distinction between them.

وَالدَّلِيلُ قَوْلُهُ تَعَالَى:

The proof is the word of Allaah:

{وَقَاتِلُوهُمْ حَتَّى لَا تَكُونَ فِتْنَةٌ وَيَكُونَ الدِّينُ كُلُّهُ لِلَّهِ}.

And fight them until there is no more Fitnah (disbelief and polytheism: i.e. worshipping others besides Allaah) and the religion (worship) will all be for Allaah Alone [in the whole of the world].

فَدَلِيلُ الشَّمْسِ وَالقَمَرِ؛ قَوْلُهُ تَعَالَى:

And the proof for (their worshipping) the sun and the moon is His (Allaah's) saying:

{وَمِنْ آيَاتِهِ اللَّيْلُ وَالنَّهَارُ وَالشَّمْسُ وَالْقَمَرُ لَا تَسْجُدُوا لِلشَّمْسِ وَلَا لِلْقَمَرِ وَاسْجُدُوا لِلَّهِ الَّذِي خَلَقَهُنَّ إِن كُنتُمْ إِيَّاهُ تَعْبُدُونَ}.

And from among His Signs are the night and the day, and the sun and the moon. Prostrate not to the sun nor to the moon but prostrate to Allaah Who created them if you (really) worship Him.

And the proof for (their worship of) the Angels is His saying:

{وَيَوْمَ يَحْشُرُهُمْ جَمِيعًا ثُمَّ يَقُولُ لِلْمَلَائِكَةِ أَهَؤُلَاءِ إِيَّاكُمْ كَانُوا يَعْبُدُونَ * قَالُوا سُبْحَانَكَ أَنتَ وَلِيُّنَا مِن دُونِهِم بَلْ كَانُوا يَعْبُدُونَ الْجِنَّ أَكْثَرُهُم بِهِم مُّؤْمِنُونَ}

And (remember) the Day when He will gather them all together, and then will say to the angels: "Was it you that these people used to worship?" They (angels) will say: "Glorified be You! You are our Walee (Lord) instead of them. Nay, but they used to worship the jinns; most of them were believers in them."

(Soorah Saba' 34: 40-41)

وَدَلِيلُ الأَنْبِيَاءِ؛ قَوْلُهُ تَعَالَى:

The proof of (their worship of) the Prophets is the saying o Allaah, The Exalted:

{وَإِذْ قَالَ اللَّهُ يَاعِيسَى ابْنَ مَرْيَمَ ءَأَنتَ قُلْتَ لِلنَّاسِ اتَّخِذُونِي وَأُمِّيَ إِلَهَيْنِ مِن دُونِ اللَّهِ قَالَ سُبْحَانَكَ مَا يَكُونُ لِي أَنْ أَقُولَ مَا لَيْسَ

لِي بِحَقٍّ}.

And (remember) when Allaah will say (on the Day
of Resurrection): "O 'Iesa (Jesus), son of Maryam
(Mary)! Did you say unto men: 'Worship me and
my mother as two gods besides Allaah?'" He will
say: "Glory be to You! It was not for me to say what
I had no right (to say)…"

[Soorah al-Maidah, Verse: 116]

وَدَلِيلُ الصَّالِحِينَ؛ قَوْلُهُ تَعَالَى:

The proof of (their worship of) the righteous is the
word of Allaah:

{قُلِ ادْعُوا الَّذِينَ زَعَمْتُم مِّن دُونِهِ فَلَا

يَمْلِكُونَ كَشْفَ الضُّرِّ عَنكُمْ وَلَا تَحْوِيلًا *
أُوْلَئِكَ الَّذِينَ يَدْعُونَ يَبْتَغُونَ إِلَى رَبِّهِمُ
الْوَسِيلَةَ أَيُّهُمْ أَقْرَبُ وَيَرْجُونَ رَحْمَتَهُ
وَيَخَافُونَ عَذَابَهُ إِنَّ عَذَابَ رَبِّكَ كَانَ
مَحْذُورًا}.

Those whom they call upon [like 'Iesa (Jesus) - son
of Maryam (Mary), 'Uzair (Ezra), angel, etc.] desire
(for themselves) means of

access to their Lord (Allāh), as to which of them
should be the nearest and they ['Iesa (Jesus), 'Uzair
(Ezra), angels, etc.] hope for His Mercy and fear His
Torment. Verily, the torment of your Lord is
something to be afraid of!

[Soorah al-israa, verse: 57]

وَدَلِيلُ الأَشْجَارِ وَالأَحْجَارِ؛ قَوْلُهُ تَعَالَى:

The proof of the trees and stones is the saying of Allaah:

{أَفَرَءَيْتُمُ اللَّاتَ وَالْعُزَّى * وَمَنَاةَ الثَّالِثَةَ الأُخْرَى}،

Have you then considered Al-Lat, and Al-'Uzza (two idols of the pagan Arabs). And Manat (another idol of the pagan Arabs), the other third?

[Soorah an-Najm, verse: 19-20]

وَحَدِيثُ أَبِي وَاقِدٍ اللَّيْثِيِّ رَضِيَ اللهُ عَنْهُ

قَالَ:

And the hadith of Abee Waaqid Al-Laythee (Allaah be pleased with him), he said:

«خَرَجْنَا مَعَ رَسُولِ اللَّهِ صَلَّى اللهُ عَلَيْهِ وَسَلَّمَ إِلَى حُنَيْنٍ وَنَحْنُ حُدَثَاءُ عَهْدٍ بِكُفْرٍ،

We went out with the Prophet ﷺ to Hunayn

and we were new to Islaam (recently come out of Kufr – Disbelief),

وَلِلْمُشْرِكِينَ سِدْرَةٌ، يَعْكُفُونَ عِنْدَهَا وَيَنُوطُونَ بِهَا أَسْلِحَتَهُمْ، يُقَالُ لَهَا: ذَاتُ أَنْوَاطٍ.

and the polytheists have a lotus tree, they use to gather around it

and they use to hang their weapons on it (to seek blessings), it (the

tree) is called; dhaat anwaat.

فَمَرَرْنَا بِسِدْرَةٍ فَقُلْنَا: يَا رَسُولَ اللَّهِ! اجْعَلْ لَنَا ذَاتَ أَنْوَاطٍ كَمَا لَهُمْ ذَاتُ أَنْوَاطٍ.

So we passed by a lotus tree and said: 'O Messenger of Allaah! Make for us a Dhaat Anwaat, just as they have a Dhaat Anwaat.'"

فَقَالَ رَسُولُ اللَّهِ صَلَّى اللهُ عَلَيْهِ وَسَلَّمَ: اللَّهُ

أَكْبَرُ! إِنَّهَا السُّنَنُ، قُلْتُمْ وَالَّذِي نَفْسِي بِيَدِهِ، كَمَا قَالَتْ بَنُو إِسْرَائِيلَ لِمُوسَى: { اجْعَل لَّنَا إِلَٰهًا كَمَا لَهُمْ آلِهَةٌ ۚ قَالَ إِنَّكُمْ قَوْمٌ تَجْهَلُونَ }.

He ﷺ said: "Allaah is the Greatest. Verily, it is a sunan (the way of the people of the past). You said—by the one in whose my soul is—just like the children of israel said to Moosaa: Make for us an ilaahan (a god) as they have aaliha (gods). He (Moosa) said: "Verily, you are a people who know not (the Majesty and Greatness of Allaah and what is obligatory upon you, i.e. to worship none but Allaah Alone, the One and the Only God of all that exists)."

[Soorah al-A'araaf, verse: 138]

القَاعِدَةُ الرَّابِعَةُ

THE FOURTH PRINCIPLE

أَنَّ مُشْرِكِي زَمَانِنَا أَغْلَظُ شِرْكاً مِنَ الأَوَّلِينَ؛

Verily, the mushrikūn (polytheists) of our time (era) are severe in (their committing of) shirk than the first (polytheist of Makkah during the Prophet's time, and those before them);

لِأَنَّ الأَوَّلِينَ يُشْرِكُونَ فِي الرَّخَاءِ وَيُخْلِصُونَ فِي الشِّدَّةِ،

this is because the old polytheists use to commit

shirk (ascribe partners to Allaah) during comfort times (times of ease), and (but) they become sincere (directing all forms of worship to Allaah) in the difficult times (during times of hardship).

وَمُشْرِكُو زَمَانِنَا شِرْكُهُمْ دَائِمٌ فِي الرَّخَاءِ وَالشِّدَّةِ.

But the polytheists of our time (era), their (committing) shirk is continuous in (both) easy and difficult times.

وَالدَّلِيلُ قَوْلُهُ تَعَالَى:

The proof is the saying of Allaah:

{فَإِذَا رَكِبُوا فِي الْفُلْكِ دَعَوُا اللَّهَ مُخْلِصِينَ لَهُ الدِّينَ فَلَمَّا نَجَّاهُمْ إِلَى الْبَرِّ إِذَا هُمْ يُشْرِكُونَ}.

And when they embark on a ship, they invoke Allāh, making their Faith pure for Him only, but when He brings them safely to land, behold, they give a share of their worship to others.

[Soorah Al-Ankaboot, verse:65].

وَاللَّهُ أَعْلَمُ.

And Allaah knows best

***

www.ingramcontent.com/pod-product-compliance
Lightning Source LLC
Chambersburg PA
CBHW030404160726

47992CB00007B/2958